The
HOPE
EQUATION

Real People, Real Change, Real Impact

JEFF
CARDWELL

with Chris Johnson

THE HOPE EQUATION
Real People, Real Change, Real Impact

Copyright © 2025 **Jeff Cardwell**

ISBN (Paperback): 979-8-89672-103-1
ISBN (Ebook): 979-8-89672-104-8

Printed in the United States of America.

5830 E 2nd St, Ste 7000 #9983
Casper, WY 82609
USA

Table of Contents

Table of Contents

It's always uplifting to visit families The People Helping People Network has helped in El Salvador.

Introduction

The People Helping People Network is a life-changing movement with many years of experience in uplifting and empowering families to go beyond merely having better lives to thriving. In the process, those around them and entire communities have been uplifted and now flourish, as well.

Our success draws upon life lessons handed down by my parents, practicality and efficiency I've learned on the job as an ambitious businessman and builder, and the skills and insight shared by the many partners who have helped power our ministry through the years. The People Helping People's mission is to build a network of people and organizations to break the cycle of poverty through housing, hunger relief, healthcare, and education initiatives as an expression of our faith. We deliver real change that empowers, sustains, and provides HOPE.

Above all, it leans upon the teachings of Jesus Christ. While our nonprofit's holistic approach to helping people help themselves has been honed and sharpened over the past couple of decades, it is also accurate to say that the solid foundation upon which it has been built is more than two millennia old.

A single moment ...

I was going 24/7. Business was booming, but I was never at home. I wasn't with my kids. I was working all the time because I thought that was what I was supposed to do. I grew up in poverty, technically speaking — although I never knew it as a child who was surrounded by loving parents who lived joyous lives of purpose. As an adult, I swore that my family would never experience any financial need. My primary mission was to provide for my family, and I thought making money would solve everything.

But a life-altering moment happened on June 17, 2000 — a date that is permanently etched into my mind and heart. A single moment that unexpectedly knocked me to my knees and sent streams of tears down my cheeks in a prayer tower in rural El Salvador.

I was a chaperone on a church mission trip that my then 11-year-old daughter Sara had insisted upon going — a journey that I very reluctantly made kicking and screaming because I was knee-deep in running successful businesses that I believed required my constant attention. That is when God opened my eyes with a gut-wrenching paradigm shift:

> *You're a good husband and father, Jeff, but you can be better. You're a good Christian, Jeff, but you can do more with your faith.*

I *felt* those words as a 15-year-old Salvadoran resident named Maria placed a purple prayer ribbon upon my neck in that prayer tower at King's Castle Ministries. The words I actually *heard* from Maria were: "I don't know what's going on in your life, but all I know is that God wants you to make time for Him in your life."

I was blind-sided. I was a churchgoer. I was tithing. I was giving to missions. Maria had spent the previous several days serving as the interpreter for the church youth group and had struck up an immediate friendship with Sara. But she didn't really know me, and she could not have possibly known that my life was as chaotic as it was. I had a false sense of security.

That moment opened my eyes. Even as I reflect upon that moment today, I still tear up. They are not tears of joy or sadness or gratitude. When you let God into your heart, something has to go out. It could be shouts of praise or joyous laughter. For me, it comes out in tears of pure, raw emotion that I could not explain then, nor today as I once again clutch this precious purple prayer ribbon.

Photo by Chris Johnson
At the Prayer Tower at King's Castle Ministries in El Salvador, you can find people praying 24 hours a day, every day of the year.

Just a few minutes before I had ascended the hill to the prayer tower, I had what I thought was a random encounter. Our church youth were in the King's Castle gymnasium with many other kids from other churches getting ready to eat and going through a briefing, *and it was loud!* I had decided to step outside and get some fresh air. I sat under a tree. Other than the faint sounds of laughter and the chirping birds, it was quiet. Then a man sat down with me. His name was Dan Carpenter from Houston, Texas and he had been at King's Castle for several months helping their founder Don Triplett build dorms and different things. I commented that it looked like he had a lot of projects going on and pointed toward one that looked like it was nearing completion.

"That one there looks like it's about finished," I said.

He had a different take. "Oh, no, it's been sitting that way for nearly a year. We're just having trouble getting the materials to finish it. It's hard to get materials down here."

I asked him what he needed, and we got up and walked through it. He needed some plumbing items, light fixtures, and numerous odds and ends. Everything he needed, I had in my warehouse back in Indianapolis. I told him if he could get me to a phone, I thought I could help get him the materials and get it finished. That's just what we did.

Looking back, that "random" encounter was when God flipped the light switch in my heart, though I didn't know it until I saw the light in the prayer tower. *That* was the genesis of The People Helping People Network. God had been preparing me all along for that moment from my youth to my rise in the business world to my first forays into charitable efforts. I could connect people in need with people who could help. I knew how to get desperately needed materials where they needed to be, where they could make a difference. I thought networking and logistics were merely business skills. I never suspected God was up to something with me as my young entrepreneurial days and career moves unfolded. I don't think God's plan was top-secret. I'm sure there were signs along the way. Maybe I just was not paying attention. Perhaps I was not meant to know His plan for me until that moment in the prayer tower. I was sure of one thing on June 17, 2000 — *everything* just changed.

I was born in the small town of Morgantown, Kentucky, but my family moved to Indianapolis when I was 2 years old. My parents were hard-working folks who instilled in me and my two older brothers (who are now deceased) solid Midwestern values and blue-collar work ethic, along with the Biblical responsibility to help others in need when possible. My dad, an Army veteran who served in Korea, was a coal miner in

Kentucky but moved the family to Indy to take a position as a welder. My mother then got a job as a nurse's aide in a nursing home.

I didn't think much about it at the time, but they both set great examples for what I do today — finding ways to help people in need. We were technically living in poverty based upon economic data points, but, again, I had no idea. My family was rich in spirit. Most importantly, my parents provided the asset that all children need to thrive — *unconditional love*. I can never thank them enough for the wealth of love that they poured not only into me and my brothers but also to every extended family member, as well as friends and even strangers. They exemplified the commandment from which so much good flows — *love thy neighbor*.

My grandmother moved in with us after my grandfather died in Kentucky, and that allowed both of my parents to work. And they worked *all the time*. Many days and nights, my mother worked double-shifts. My father worked long days for 40 years at the same little welding shop in Indianapolis. After dinner, he would tackle side jobs in our garage. He was an expert diesel mechanic, and our church bus was always breaking down, so he was constantly giving back to our congregation by working on the bus. My mom held almost continuous rummage and yard sales. She would get stuff donated by other people and sell it — and all of the proceeds went to church missions. From time to time, there were missionaries and other guests who would come to our church, and we would host them at our house. I doubt that they had any idea that we were technically poor as they were lavished with love and hospitality.

My mother then went to school to become an LPN and then spent the rest of her career working at the state mental hospital. She would take all of the hand-me-down clothes from me and my brothers to the hospital because she said those patients and kids never had anything. Many of them had no one to visit them or show concern from the outside, and she treated them as if they were her own family.

My parents were always reaching out and helping others when many times they really could have used some help themselves. It's only now as I look back that I realize the sacrifices they were making not just for me and my brothers but for so many people in need. Always reaching out to help others was the legacy they instilled in me by the power of their example.

As I grew up, I was doing all kinds of odd jobs. Of course, I had a paper route, and that was always fun, especially around the month of May with the Indianapolis 500. Selling papers at the Indianapolis Motor Speedway during the month of May was a big deal. You could make all kinds of money as a kid as we rode bikes up and down the line of people waiting to get into the racetrack. That was our Christmas in May. Of course, like many kids, I cut a lot of grass, too. My mom and dad bought me that lawnmower so I could earn extra money.

During my school days, we had trades and industrial arts. I took welding, automobile maintenance, and woodworking, and different career education. And I really enjoyed all of it.

My first real job, though, was part-time in a print shop, and per-haps — again, looking back — there was a rather obvious clue that I missed that God was working on me and my future. We printed many, *many* pictures of Jesus Christ — the well-known Warner Salmon paintings of Jesus by Kriebel and Bates, which was based in Indianapolis but whose work is around the world. My job was to take the lithographs and put them onto hard cardboard backing. I ran the glue machine and did that after school.

Then I got a job that would be the first rung on a very tall ladder that I would climb on the way to my current career in the hardware and building supply business.

I got a job on a framing crew for house construction, although I was merely the gopher. Every time they were out of something, I'd be the one who ran to the lumber yard. When things began to slow down in construction, the lumber yard was hiring. They had seen me darting in and out all the time picking up stuff, and they gave me a job. That's how I got started, part-time, at 15 years old in the lumber and building materials business.

Meanwhile, I earned enough credits in high school to graduate as a junior, and the lumber yard gave me a full-time job. I've been in some variation of building and construction ever since.

During my first full-time years at the lumber yard, I bought an old beatup dump truck and spent many nights earning extra money doing clean-up for construction crews after work. Then I started doing insulation in some of the crawl spaces of the new homes at night. I did a number of odds and ends to make extra money. Thank goodness I was a teenager with plenty of young energy!

When I was 18, the manager of the lumber yard decided to retire. I was an ambitious kid and threw my hat into the ring for the job. The manager was in his 70s, but the owner decided out of the blue to give this ambitious kid a chance. Was I that impressive or was no one else crazy enough to want it? I do not know. That was 1978. Then, in 1980, business fell like a rock. Interest rates were through the roof. We were in total survival mode, but we pushed through.

The owner at the time, Don Huddleston, was always very good to me, but he spent winters in Florida. Here I was, 20 years old in 1980, and he headed to Florida in January and stayed until April and left it all up to me, a kid. He'd called to check in, but things kept going well. We managed to work through the rough times and began growing once again.

By 1985, business was booming, and we were *busy*. Don left again that January, and I told him that I had aspirations to someday own the company. He supported the concept, though I didn't have any money to really invest at the time. But I refinanced the house and bought a stake before he went to Florida. I managed to get 5 percent of the company, and we were going to put together some sort of contract buyout program when he got back.

But he got sick that spring down in Florida and was not doing well. He came home in April to see his own doctors and found out he needed gallbladder surgery. After that, he had an aneurysm, and on May 12 of that year he passed away. We never had that conversation about a buyout and never had anything in writing. By default, that made me partners with his wife, Barb, whom I'd only met a few times. Yet, it blossomed into a fantastic alliance. Don had really kept his personal and business life separate, so she knew he did well financially but had no idea the extent of his investments and properties beyond the lumber yard. I began to manage those, and it piqued my interest in real estate.

I had married Cheryl the year before, and she wanted to sell real estate. I wanted to learn more about real estate with Don having so many properties. So, we both went to real estate school to get our licenses.

That went well for us, and Cheryl was doing fantastic selling homes. Then we got our broker's licenses, and we found a really good niche. I loved the real estate business, so I started doing the same thing Don had done earlier on — buying real estate on the side and having rental property investments.

Then, I was able to buy a bit of ground and wanted to do a small subdivision. The man whom I'd worked for in the framing business, Mike Gorman, was still our best customer at the lumber yard. I called him and suggested we partner up to build the subdivision's houses ourselves. We had a five-year plan to build out this small subdivision, and we sold it out in about a year and a half. So, that was a huge success.

Then, Don had a farm on the southside that was 20-something acres, and Barb suggested we do a subdivision there and add it to the partnership.

We had a three-way partnership — me, Mike and Barb. In Don's memory, we named it Huddleston Estates. It was a really big project for us that we thought would take five to seven years to do. That was 1988, and by 1990 it was full. Then we built office spaces that we still have called Huddleston Professional Centre. So, we had great success in house building and real estate, and the lumber business was good. Things were booming. All was well.

About the same time we were building Huddleston Estates, Habitat for Humanity came to Indianapolis. In 1992, they approached us at the store wanting in-kind donations. We were a small lumber yard, but we managed to donate what we could.

Then, they got with Mike one on one. Mike's very aggressive, a risk-taker. We were an odd couple when it came to building. I was a very reserved, conservative and pragmatic guy. We were good for each other because I kind of held him back from walking right off the plank, while he kind of dragged me onto the plank a little bit when I didn't want to take another step. We really balanced each other. One day the executive director of the local Habitat said that, "You guys have been very helpful. Now, you guys need to sponsor a house." And, of course, Mike said he thought we could do that.

He came to me, and I was like, "No way." We were donating some materials already, and I told him I just didn't think we would be able to do that. But he insisted he would get everyone on board and get our subs to participate and donate and talked me into it even though I thought we were biting off way more than we could chew. Looking back at that and the first trip to El Salvador, I'm amazed how many things I was dragged into "kicking and screaming" that changed my life for the better. Thank God for the people who have refused to take my "no's" for an answer!

So, we did it. We built the Habitat house, and it was a great success. It was a lot of fun. All of our subs came in. All of our framers and electricians joined the effort. Everyone pitched in. We raised the money and built it for very little cash. Most everything was in-kind donations because we were booming and building so many other houses that everybody was glad to jump on board and help. We just had so much fun, and that was really when I got hooked — hooked on getting involved.

The next year, Habitat was really wanting to make their presence known, and they decided to build 10 houses … in one week! I had a lot of connections in the real estate business, and Mike was a third-generation builder who knew a lot of other builders. I looked up to him. He was 10 years older than me and a good friend. He was a high-quality guy, and I loved him like my own brother really. When they came to us and said they wanted us to lead that 10-home build, of course Mike said, "Sure! We'll do it!" Again, it sounded like a bit much to me, but I trusted him enough to walk right back out on that plank once again merely grumbling a little under my breath but not kicking and screaming for a change!

About that same time, a good friend had a radio show and wanted me to come on the air and talk about this blitz build. I'd appear on his weekly show and give him updates about it and recruit volunteers and support.

Mike started talking to the Builders Association and getting other builders involved. We'd just finished that one house a year earlier, so we knew we could do another house on our own. What we needed to do was get nine other builders involved and have them do the same thing. That's exactly what we did! We got 10 crews out, 10 builders and all kinds of volunteers. I recruited lots of volunteers through the radio. We had more volunteers than we actually needed, a wonderful problem to have when doing nonprofit work.

This actually launched me into doing regular radio. I was on the air doing those updates all the time. And for whatever reason,. They kept inviting me back. The next thing I knew I had my own radio show from 1994 to 2014.

During this blitz build, Millard Fuller (who founded Habitat for Humanity in 1976 and The Fuller Center for Housing in 2005) came up. I had the honor of working side-by-side with him on that build. It was like we had known each other all our lives. It was a lot of fun, and we had a great time. It became an incredible friendship. Millard became one of my greatest inspirations and my mentor.

Millard handled the dedication ceremony for the house that we built. My church was also involved in the build. It was such a special moment turning over the keys to the homeowner. There wasn't a dry eye on the lot. Afterward, they passed out awards and such. I have received many awards over the years — nice awards that obviously cost a lot of money, beautiful trophies, and different things. And one of the most cherished "awards" I have is this one right here:

Photo by Jeff Cardwell

I'd been hooked a year earlier, but now I was completely reeled in. I witnessed so much in a short period of time. It was so rewarding to play a part in fulfilling a dream for a family. It was a fulfilling experience for every volunteer and every single person on the job site. I learned a lot from Millard that week and would learn even more in the years to come.

One of the biggest things was building on faith — requiring me to slightly loosen up with my practical, pragmatic nature. When we first started that week, we certainly didn't have all the resources we needed to complete it. I remember Millard brushing it off and saying that's the way it is on every job — you just gotta work through it, take a leap of faith, and God will provide. Um, OK. But that's just what happened! Anything we needed would show up right when we needed it.

I didn't have the type of faith that Millard had. Few people ever have had such faith. But, to see his confidence that somehow, some way God would provide was really inspiring to me. I was more apt to pour over the plan and examine scenarios, but Millard would just dive right in. It was true faith in action. It taught me a valuable lesson about trusting God, though it stretched me a lot. It still stretches me even today. I guess we are all still works in progress.

After that blitz with Millard, I was always looking for opportunities to get involved in helping others. I was sitting on the local board of Habitat. We developed some subdivisions that were Habitat-only. I remember how big of an event it was when we reached the 100-house mark for Habitat in Indy, and then Indiana's First Lady Judy O'Bannon came down, and we became good friends even though we had different politics. That's when I began to see how Millard's Theology of the Hammer worked, bringing people from all walks of life together for a common cause. That's what I love most about mission work today — that uniting force, especially in times of division and polarization.

The O'Bannons remained good friends, and they were close with Millard and Linda Fuller. When Millard died in 2009, which was after Frank had died in 2003, Judy called and asked if we were going to Millard's memorial service in Atlanta and asked if she could tag along with me and my mother. We were so thankful to have Judy join us. The memorial service held at Atlanta's famed Ebenezer Baptist Church, once led by Martin Luther King Jr., was a true celebration of life. It was held a little more than a month after a somber burial in an unmarked grave at historic Koinonia Farm near Americus, Georgia, as Millard had requested. Millard would have preferred the joyous memorial service. There were some tears, but there were more smiles as people remembered his enthusiasm for life and his determination to build a better world.

The hammer brings people together. When we enter the mission field, we all lose our titles and become equal. Everybody is focused on the common goal of helping somebody in need. It gets you out of the fastpaced money-making world and the to-do lists that you can never seem to finish. I was beginning to realize that I thrived in the kind of environment in which effective, driven, busy nonprofits operate. It was so gratifying to me to be around like-minded people, even more so when you're working alongside folks that you may never have otherwise gotten to know in our silos of everyday life and politics and business.

I had been hooked. I had been reeled in. I was caught and released back into a sea of good will where I was content to keep swimming in the safe waters, the shallow end. But God was about to get hold of me in ways I never imagined and throw me into the deep waters, — in a place I never imagined ever being because I never thought I was qualified. I wasn't a missionary. I wasn't a pastor. I wasn't a doctor. I was a businessman.

PHP Network file photo
One of my many return trips to King's Castle in El Salvador was in 2006 with my mother Betty Cardwell, son Jeffery, and daughter Sara.

If it had been up to me, I'd have never been there in that prayer tower in El Salvador for God to knock me to my knees. But it wasn't up to me.

Thank God.

El Salvador

For years, El Salvador has been the proving ground for The People Helping People Network's model of charity and, specifically, The HOPE Equation that I will discuss shortly. However, I never whipped out a map and threw a dart to randomly select a country in which to work. I didn't *choose* El Salvador.

El Salvador chose me.

The seed for that trip was planted back in 1990 when Dr. Michael Elmore gave a presentation at Parc-Way Assembly of God, where my wife Cheryl was a fourth.-generation member. I did not know Dr. Elmore very well, but I found myself inspired as he shared slides from his first mission trip abroad to Guatemala. He passionately shared stories of his mission trip and emanated a Millard-esque enthusiasm for service. He had found a way to merge his medical gifts as a doctor by putting his faith in action in the mission field abroad. I nudged Cheryl:

"Now, *that's* adventure travel! I'd love to do that someday."

It was a nice thought, but I did not think I could contribute in a way remotely close to what Dr. Elmore could do. He provided life-saving medical care and crucial screenings. He had expertise that made an immediate difference in people's lives. At least with my housing connections there were ways for me to meaningfully contribute in the Indianapolis area. And I was able to do just that through the decade to come. What I didn't realize, though, was that Dr. Elmore had planted a seed in my heart that day at Parc-Way. It was buried deep but fertilized throughout the 1990s with the help of many good-hearted folks. Come 2000, a new year and a new millennium, that seed was getting ready to sprout, unbeknownst to me.

My headstrong, independent daughter came home from Parc-Way with an inspiration. Parc-Way's youth group was going on a mission trip to El Salvador in June. Though she was only 11 years old and not officially old enough to be in the youth group, she was invited to go. She was mature for her age, independent and determined. She wanted to go. I said, "Sure, you can go." Business was good, and it wasn't that expensive of a trip. "Sounds great!"

Well, when we got home and told my wife, Cheryl was furious. "YOU DID WHAT?!"

Cardwell family photo
With my daughter Sara during that fateful 2000 trip to El Salvador.

I told her that the youth pastor, Kevin Stewart, would take care of her. She was friends with older girls on the trip who would look out for her. She'd be fine, I assured her. Cheryl was not happy — to put it mildly — that I was willing to send our daughter off to a third-world country at 11 years old.

"You're gonna have to go with her," she said.

No. No. No. There was *no way* I could go. They were going in June, and we had several houses under construction. The lumber yard was booming, and we were beyond busy. You've got to make hay while the sun is shining, I argued.

A few weeks went by, and the Cardwell home was not a happy place.

On a Friday morning the Sunday before the group was to leave, I got a call from Pastor Kevin. He wanted to come by my office to talk to me. I figured they were probably short-handed on funds and needed a little money for the trip. I figured I could help out with that.

The first thing he said when he walked into my office was that he didn't need any money. He told me that two of the chaperones were in an auto accident that morning. Thankfully, their injuries were relatively minor, but they wouldn't be able to go to El Salvador. Kevin said he could make do with the four chaperones he had remaining, but he could really use one more adult. He started thinking about who at the church had a passport and could get away in short notice. He said that was a short list, and I was on it. Again, I explained just how busy June was for me and the business. Kevin knew that I never left home without my calendar and asked to see it. I said it was still in the car.

"Jeff," he said, "let's go out to your vehicle, but make me a promise before we walk out there: If those dates in your calendar are empty, will you go to El Salvador with us?"

I told him that would be a miracle. We went to my car, and, surely enough, the next week was blank. Did I forget to pencil in my appointments? Did someone sneak into my book and erase them? Whatever the case, I was busted!

"Did you talk to God before this?" I asked him.

Kevin asked me to pray on it — but do it quickly. I went home and prayed about it. I'm not sure whether I received a subtle sign from above, but I am quite certain about the crystal-clear command I got from Cheryl.

"Oh, you're definitely going now!"

Sometimes when forces begin aligning against you, you just have to assess the situation honestly and admit defeat. They had won. That didn't mean I had to be happy about it, and I wasn't. When I say I went on that first El Salvador trip "kicking and screaming," it's only a slight exaggeration. Boarding the plane, I prayed that the youth would have an enlightening trip and be spiritually moved — and that I could get this over with as quickly as possible.

The trip was in conjunction with King's Castle Ministries, led by Don Triplett. I knew very little about this organization that Don launched in El Salvador back when it was mired in a brutal civil war. He never intended to have an extended stay in the country. He had been on his way to Nicaragua but was unable to enter the country. Apparently, as I have witnessed in my own journey, God had other plans for him. Don planted roots in El Salvador, and now his ministry with its primary mission of training missionaries to share the Gospel of Jesus Christ has gone international.

PHP Network file photo
Visiting children in El Salvador in 2006 with my son Jeffery and Maria.

King's Castle assigned Maria Mercedes de Cruz to serve as our interpreter and guide during our week-plus in the country. Maria had moved to Canada when she was 6 to escape the civil war and then returned with the family five years later when it was safe. As someone who had one foot planted in Central America and another in North America with fluency in both Spanish and English, Maria's presence was invaluable. She fit right in with our youth group, but no individual connection was stronger than the one she forged with my daughter, Sara. Maria was just 15 but mature beyond her years. She took Sara under her wing, and they remain friends today.

Maria was a calming presence on the bus, and she had no shortage of opportunities to translate as we encountered many speedbumps — several members of our group got sick, one was bitten by a poisonous spider, the bus got temporarily stuck in a mudslide, and guerrillas surrounded our bus in one heart-stopping encounter. Even then, there was a moment of levity as Sara believed gorillas were about to board the bus, something we still laugh about today. Maria's maturity and leadership got us through all of those sticky situations.

Then came the moment at King's Castle's prayer tower. As I noted before, I was overwhelmed emotionally. Maybe it had something to do with getting away from the norm — far away from the day-to-day grind of the many businesses back home. Perhaps it was just the culmination of all we had witnessed in El Salvador from the third-world poverty conditions to meeting the caring souls at orphanages and relief centers who had committed their lives to helping people in need. Whatever led to that moment, it was unmistakable that God had grabbed my heart. I was being called to do more, and God dispatched me to El Salvador for a reason. When God grabbed my heart, He clearly left part of it on the ground in that country. I *love* El Salvador — the land, the food, and, most of all, the people. They needed help, but even the people who lived in shacks and who had very little food or money had a joy that I did not understand. They had

Photo by Todd Scoggins
It's always good to revisit Don Triplett at King's Castle, as I got to do in December 2022.

potential. They had faith. What they needed more than anything was *hope*.

"I think when you look at things through God's eyes, that's when you fall in love with something," Maria would later tell The People Helping People Network about that first trip. "I think that's what happened with Jeff. He didn't realize it at the time, but what he was seeing was something through God's eyes. God sometimes just moves that veil from our eyes and we see something that we never thought we would see. I think that's what happened to him on that trip."

"Jeff came in here just willing to help, and then the Lord got hold of him," Don recalled of that first trip when I and a team of People Helping People Network supporters met him and revisited King's Castle and its prayer tower back in December 2022. "God takes an event that happens in our lives and turns it into a cause. If we can discover our purpose, it's unbelievable what the Lord can do. He got hit by a cause bigger than himself."

The prayer tower at King's Castle is the highest point on the King's Castle campus and provides a stunning view of picturesque Lake Coatepeque, a 10-square-mile crater natural reservoir formed by an ancient volcanic eruption. The lava and rock formations have made this deep lake a popular and exotic scuba diving location. While divers descend to undiscovered depths of the lake, others are ascending the hill to King's Castle's prayer tower that is occupied every day — 24 hours a day, every single minute, every day of the year — by prayerful souls. Some quietly reflect. Others are vocal in their passion. Each member of our 20-person group was touched when we revisited that tower on December 3, 2022. Again,

I felt God's presence. I was emotional. It was here that the seeds for the life-changing, yet simple HOPE Equation were first planted. I'm hardly the first person who has had an epiphany in that tower.

"I think in those moments, God just comes and puts that mustard seed in your heart, and it grows into a great big tree," Don later told us. "I think that's what this is really all about."

Don is now both a spiritual mentor and a good friend. Maria would return to Canada, and we consider her to be part of the

Cardwell family. She is grateful that The People Helping People Network has made El Salvador its proving ground for the basics of effective charity that empowers and uplifts.

"I think it's a country that has great, hard-working, loving people," Maria says of El Salvador. "I think because of situations that have happened like the civil war and natural disasters that sometimes has set people back. But if you give them the tools and point them in the right direction, they are always willing to work. And they're so thankful. I find that to be a quality in my people."

The trip upon which I was dragged "kicking and screaming" changed my life. Now, I'm more likely to be kicking and screaming these days if something gets in the way of my going back to El Salvador every year — multiple times most years. Sara has made multiple visits, as well, as has my son Jeffery, who made his first mission trip to El Salvador in 2006 at the age of 10. They both remain actively involved in People Helping People Network operations and leadership. My wife Cheryl and mother Betty also have visited the country. They all know first-hand that this a beautiful country full of wonderful people..

The seeds of our nonprofit work and the life-transforming HOPE Equation were planted there. A natural disaster spurred those seeds to begin sprouting less than six months later.

"You're listening to The People Helping People Network"

So, how did I come up with "The People Helping People Network" as the name for our nonprofit? In short, I didn't.

The radio show that had sprung from my original appearances to promote the 10-house blitz build in 1994 had morphed into a call-in show in which I'd answer questions about real estate. I talked about Habitat throughout the years, but I talked mostly about real estate issues.

When I got back from that first trip to El Salvador, I went to the station manager — Ed Roehling, a good friend who was inducted into the Indiana Broadcast Pioneers Hall of Fame in 2016 — and told him that I was done with radio and was ready to wrap it up. I was getting the same questions all the time, and I thought the show had run its course.

He said, "No, no. We want to keep you on the air. What do you want to do?"

I said, "Oh, I don't know, Ed. I don't really know what I want to do. There's more important things in life than people fixing up and repairing their homes. Ed, life is really all about people helping people. I want to do something to really help people."

He said, "Hey! That would be a great show!" "What do you mean?" I asked.

"*People Helping People!* That sounds good! Do a show about that! You wanna help people, so let's do *The People Helping People Network.*"

26

The next week, we started The People Helping People Network. My very first guest actually was Gen. Chuck Yeager. He was in Indianapolis for a private event, and he agreed to do a taping for the show. We taped on Tuesday, September 4, 2001 — exactly one week before 9/11.

I started inviting nonprofits to talk about their work on an hour-long show. One week, it'd be The American Red Cross, then The Salvation Army, Boy Scouts and Girl Scouts. Any of the area nonprofits, I had them on. I had Millard Fuller on several times, and we'd talk about Habitat for Humanity and then later on The Fuller Center for Housing.

On January 13, 2001, a 7.8-magnitude earthquake struck El Salvador with its epicenter 90 miles east of the bustling capital of San Salvador. More than 169,000 houses were damaged, and more than 5,500 people were injured. At least 944 people were killed, including Maria's dear aunt, who perished in a quake-triggered landslide. I wanted to help in any way I could, and we brought Maria to Indiana to stay with us for a couple of weeks so she could share her story and encourage people to help affected families in El Salvador. The local response was overwhelmingly supportive — to the surprise of absolutely no one who is familiar with the generous spirit of those who live in America's heartland.

Before long, we had containers of supplies going to help quake victims in El Salvador. I had fallen in love with El Salvador months earlier, but now there was a specific call to action. Connections were being cemented that ultimately would pave the way for the accomplishments of today. The more we helped families in El Salvador, the more needs we discovered and the more connections we made to help address those needs. Through these partners, we were helping families find better places to live, fostering educational opportunities and economic advancement, delivering clean water, and feeding the hungry. A holistic method of facilitating uplifting and lasting transformation was in its infancy, though it was not an official plan or a named formula at the time. It was more organic. Looking back,

I now know those were the beginnings of the yet-unnamed HOPE Equation that we now specifically promote through The People Helping People Network.

The radio program proved to be a remarkably effective awareness and fundraising tool, particularly when another natural disaster struck in 2005— much closer to home this time. Katrina delivered a real gut punch to the Gulf Coast, and the tragic images unfolding on everyone's television screens moved listeners, friends, churches, and the whole community to fill warehouses with relief supplies. But they weren't doing any good in Indiana. We had to get them South — immediately.

I knew that my friend Bud Probasco was on the ground in the disaster zone almost before Katrina had moved on. As a man of action and a minister, Bud knew that, "With God, all things are possible." Then again, I have managed to test that belief a few times — especially during the Katrina relief mission. I called Bud with what I thought was pretty good news.

"I've got a 747 heading your way with supplies," I told him.

He thought I'd lost my mind! He said they didn't have power, forklifts or a fully operational airport. But he didn't have time to address my mental state — a plane was already in the air and on the way. He contacted the University of Southern Mississippi for help, and soon two lines of vehicles with their headlights on created a makeshift runway. Athletes from Southern Miss' football and basketball teams showed up to unload the plane.

"I don't know what he expected of me, but I wanna tell you this — and Jeff would say the same thing: God did it," Bud would later recall of that stressful time. "That's how we unloaded it and got it to the places it needed to be."

Bud was reassured yet again that — some way, somehow — God will provide the resources when people are in dire need, and The People Helping People Network would be ready to help deliver those resources, by truckloads and planeloads. We have since worked together on multiple disaster relief efforts through the years. And I'm sure he has muttered an urgent prayer or two after getting off the phone with me!

Fuller Center for Housing photo
Volunteers raise the wall on a new Fuller Center for
Housing home in Shreveport, La., in 2006.

Katrina would ultimately play a major role in the formation of our partnership with The Fuller Center for Housing. Millard Fuller had clashed with his board at Habitat for Humanity, ultimately leading to the firing of both he and wife Linda. Millard was down, but he was not the type to mope for very long. He was a spry 70 years old and said he could not find the word "retirement" anywhere in the Bible, so he formed The Fuller Center for Housing at first to support Habitat affiliates around the nation. He was fantastic at going into these communities and drumming up excitement and funds for their work. For some unknown reason, the invites stopped abruptly, as if someone had intervened to thwart his efforts. Then, a phone call came from Community Renewal's Mack McCarter in Shreveport, Louisiana. Thousands of refugees from Katrina were in town, and they didn't want to go home. They would need places to live. Mack immediately thought of Millard.

Millard went to Shreveport to assess the situation. One of the neighborhoods he saw was Allendale. Houses were dilapidated, vacant or home to illicit activities. Crime was rampant, fueled by drugs and hopelessness.

Millard was warned by some officials not to work there. It was beyond hope, they said, and they could not guarantee the safety of volunteers. That made the decision easy for Millard.

"This is exactly where we're going to work!" Millard declared, much to the surprise of officials in Shreveport but not the least bit of a shock to those of us who knew him well. Millard saw no person, no family, no community, nor any situation as hopeless. He vowed to restore hope to Allendale.

The Fuller Center began building its first U.S. homes there in 2005, and we sent a busload of volunteers — including my mother Betty — to work at the Millard and Linda Fuller Blitz Build in Allendale in 2006. We had a blast building together once again and delivering hope.

(Dozens of Fuller Center homes later, violent crime would drop by 83 percent over the next few years. Today, as of this writing, Allendale is a neighborhood of choice for those seeking affordable and safe places to live ... and to raise their children. We saw a similar crime decrease after the 2010 Millard Fuller Legacy Build in Indianapolis ...at which my wife and mother also volunteered!)

Millard asked me to join the Board of Directors of The Fuller Center for Housing in 2005, and, of course, I said yes. After the success in Shreveport, we were looking to have an international Fuller Center board meeting. By that time, I was already going to El Salvador every year, and I was promoting The People Helping People Network's programs in El Salvador to everybody on the Fuller Center board. So, Millard said, "OK, let's go to El Salvador and meet." Ultimately, we decided not only to hold the board meeting in El Salvador in 2008 but also another Fuller Center blitz build there at the same time. The first 16 homes in the El Salvador partnership between PHP and FCH went up that year. Again, to the surprise of no one — except for perhaps a few Salvadoran families who were not used to seeing so many Americans in one village — the build was tremendously successful. Millard loved blitz build weeks, but none of us knew at the time that it would be his last-ever blitz.

Just as we do today on The People Helping People Network's Vision Trips to El Salvador, I took Millard around during that build and showed him the children's hospital, some places where we had beds and mattresses for kids and different things, and did some food distribution. As I told Millard, "This is the work we do at People Helping People. It's more than houses." He loved the holistic approach of what was possible after the houses were built. That's when it all came together and showed us how real, transformative, lasting change was possible. The house is the foundation stone upon which human development occurs, but we've also got to get them food, get them medicine, and education so that they can sustain themselves and pay for the homes.

(The Fuller Center for Housing builds in partnership with families, offering a hand-up instead of a hand-out. Partner families repay the costs of the homes through zero-percent-interest mortgages with the repayments staying in the community to be recycled, helping family after family get the same hand-up. That's the formula of enlightened charity that Millard Fuller had developed in the late 1960s and early 1970s at Koinonia Farm with theologian Clarence Jordan. The Fuller Center continues to follow those principles of enlightened charity today, and we at The People Helping People Network have learned a thing or two from Millard's vision.)

That was the real birth of The HOPE Equation. The idea was developing. We had not coined the term or marketed it. There was no graphic explaining it. But the concept had informally and organically become a *formula*. It would soon have a name — one around which all of our work at The People Helping People Network is now centered.

The HOPE Equation

Not long after that blitz build in El Salvador, Millard Fuller died of an aortic aneurysm on Feb. 3, 2009. He was just 74 years old. He had worked that day at The Fuller Center for Housing's international headquarters in Americus, Georgia, only to go home a little early complaining that he was not feeling well. That was unusual. Millard did not like to take any time off, and he was never one to complain. No one knew how seriously ill he was, including Millard himself.

Amid the shock, the idea was briefly raised that The Fuller Center for Housing was born with Millard and that perhaps it should die with him. That notion was tossed aside quickly. Ultimately, we decided that the best way to honor Millard's life's work was to press on and chase his dream of ending poverty housing. David Snell was Millard's right-hand man at The Fuller Center, and they had worked together since the early 1990s when David organized a couple of Jimmy and Rosalynn Carter Work Projects for Habitat for Humanity. They again worked together from the first days of The Fuller Center in 2005. We unanimously chose David to be the new president of The Fuller Center.

I doubt there could have been anyone better to follow in Millard's footsteps than David Snell, who has become a dear friend and a frequent travel partner in El Salvador for Fuller Center and People Helping People Network purposes. He also is fluent in Spanish. That is particularly helpful for me because despite all of my travels in El Salvador, my language learning skills have proven to be woefully inadequate. Millard would be proud of how David has guided the ministry with a steady hand while staying true to the principles upon which The Fuller Center was founded, principles shaped decades earlier at Georgia's historic Koinonia Farm with the inspiration of Clarence Jordan. They are simple, grass-roots, Christian principles, and, most importantly, they work. The PHP-FCH partnership is natural and permanent.

Fuller Center for Housing photo
David Snell chats with former President Jimmy Carter (left) and Millard Fuller at the 1995 Jimmy and Rosalynn Carter Work Project in Los Angeles as the former First Lady looks on.

Millard's death also further steeled my resolve to continue honing our holistic approach to uplifting families and entire communities through The People Helping People Network. And, yes, part of being intentional in that holistic approach was giving it a name — The HOPE Equation.

The HOPE Equation is not exactly Einstein's Theory of Relativity.

Then, again, the beauty of The HOPE Equation is in its simplicity. Simply put, this is it:

multiplied by faith =

Just as I have served terms on the board of The Fuller Center for Housing, David has done the same for The People Helping People Network.

He also sees it as a natural relationship — and one that makes good sense from his nonprofit's point of view.

"We here at The Fuller Center know how to get houses built and we're good at it," David said. "But there are so many other needs that the people we serve have that go beyond housing — food, access to doctors, a life-preparatory education. To provide these things we look to others who know how to do them as well as we know how to build.

"People Helping People is the perfect companion ministry to The Fuller Center," he adds. "Their Hope Equation — Housing + Hunger Relief + Healthcare + Education multiplied by Faith = Hope — tells the story. The house is just the beginning. People need to eat. They need to take care of their health. They need a good job to support their families. A decent home is the platform for these basic needs and taking care of these needs allows them to be better homeowners, to afford the house and to maintain it."

Dr. Elmore, a PHP board member and long-time supporters, was the first to plant the seed of international service in my head back in the early 1990s, and he remains active in our work. He has seen how communities have flourished in El Salvador — starting with the first blocks of Fuller Center homes, followed by the infrastructure and supporting programs that make for happy and healthy communities.

"We're now able to build communities in cooperative partnerships," he said. "Now they say they don't just live in a *bario* — they live in a *colonia*, a community. There are lights at night, they have water in their homes, they have septic systems. I've always said that if you want to solve 90 percent of the health care problems in those places, give them (bathroom facilities) and give them clean water to drink. Our housing projects have done that. And People Helping People has a variety of medical services that continue to expand.

"We've always said that from an education standpoint that hungry kids living in a bad situation can't learn," he continued. "So now they're in their own safe home, and we've eliminated 90 percent of their health problems."

"I'm a health care guy, but I've always enjoyed partnering and doing the other things, as well, with housing and hunger and education," said Dr. Rick Jackson, a retired orthopedic surgeon and dedicated supporter told us. "That's a great equation to have. It doesn't hinge on one thing. When you have all of them together, it makes it more comprehensive. I didn't even realize that until Jeff came along and presented that. I thought it was a great idea. I could help with the medical part, and he was partnering with others to do the housing and other parts of it. But we all kind of work together, which makes it fun."

PHP Network file photo
A volunteer and child plant a tree in the Ahuachapán community.

Another supporter from the healthcare front is Dr. Chuck Dietzen, founder of Timmy Global Health, a People Helping People Network partner. Dr. Chuck has been honored with a PHP Servant's Heart Award, as well as the Kiwanis World Service Medal, an honor bestowed upon the likes of one of his greatest inspirations, Mother Teresa. He approves of the concept of The HOPE Equation, but he jokingly says he is a little jealous of our name, The People Helping People Network.

"I've joked with Jeff that I wish I'd named my organization People Helping People because people get locked into this idea of what a mission is, and I just like the idea of people helping people," Dr. Dietzen said. "This world, this life, is about empowerment. It's whatever I can do to help you, whatever resources I have, I'm willing to share them. What gives anything value is the ability to share it."

Simply put, The HOPE Equation works. Former Vice President Mike Pence, with whom I served as the Director of Indiana's Office of FaithBased and Community Initiatives and Senior Advisor during his term as governor, addressed our 2022 Servant's Heart Award Gala by video and did an outstanding job of summing up why The HOPE Equation is such a powerful tool for transformation — something I knew but had not quite put into these words that my friend used.

"When you address those basic necessities, as People Helping People does, you provide the foundation people need to improve their lives and build a better world," the former vice president told the crowd in a unifying message in the wake of a time of great division. "Better still, you give them the tools for people to help themselves — and that is truly transformational.

"Whether it's building homes in communities in El Salvador or responding to disasters right here in the United States and so many points in between, what People Helping People truly delivers is the one thing none of us can do without — and that's hope."

Empowerment and hope go hand-in-hand. There is a time for handouts in the charity process, but it is when you are able to extend a hand-UP that lives truly begin to change. That is when charity cases become partners and when case workers become co-workers. That's the concept of Enlightened Charity that Millard Fuller learned back in the 1960s at Koinonia. As Millard was a mentor to me, Clarence was a mentor to him. Their concepts of *partnering* with those in need, offering a hand-UP instead of a handout, led to the affordable housing movement and simply made good sense. The HOPE Equation begins with Housing, and we think that simply makes good sense.

Housing

With Millard Fuller — one of the most inspiring people
I've ever known — in Shreveport in 2007.

*"A house is the foundation stone upon which human
development occurs."*

Millard uttered that phrase many times. I honestly cannot verify whether he originated that phrase or merely adapted it from the many great thinkers who inspired him, but it also has become part of my own lexicon.

Our primary partner in housing is The Fuller Center for Housing. They believe that all of God's people ought to have a simple, decent place to call home. Homeowner families are full partners in the building process, contributing "sweat equity" hours as they build alongside volunteers and local laborers. They then repay the costs of construction on terms they can afford, over time, with zero-percent interest, no-profit mortgages. The sweat equity and repayments help partner families retain their dignity, something that often is robbed from those who are given handouts.

Not only do they retain their dignity, but they become givers themselves. Their repayments go into a Fund for Humanity and stay in their local community to help others get the same hand-UP into simple, decent homes. That basic process is the same for Fuller Center covenant partners across the United States and around the world.

"When you just give folks stuff, they tend not to appreciate it," Fuller Center President David Snell has said. "It's just human nature. And the more you give folks, the more they want. Ultimately, they wind up hating the one that's giving it to them — it's a strange dynamic, but we see it play out over and over again. I think we're being very Christian because the charity that we are engaged in is an uplifting charity."

Some, though, have wondered if such a system would work in the third world. That was a valid concern. After all, many American organizations have parachuted into the third world with well-intentioned handouts that exacerbated cultures of dependency over the decades rather than enhancing independent spirit and facilitating empowerment. However, even in the Western Hemisphere's poorest nation, Haiti, Fuller Center homes are now being built with repayments from homeowner partner families who moved from the most pitiful shacks to simple, yet quite beautiful homes. The building starts with donations and partners, but it truly accelerates when those gifts become recycled through homeowner repayments to help family after family after family. It is a rather inspired form of "charity."

A similar thing is happening in El Salvador, albeit on a much larger scale. We had been partnering with The Fuller Center for several years to build dozens of homes in various communities. Then, in 2016, a fledgling nonprofit called New Story Charity delivered a huge influx of donations to build not just homes but entire communities. First, 99 homes went up in Nuevo Cuscatlán, then 91 in Ahuachapán, 64 in El Espino, 55 in Ahuachapán II, 131 in Nuevo Cuscatlán II, and … well, I think you get the picture.

Photo by Chris Johnson
We visited Juáyua in December 2022 just before
the 50 new homes were dedicated.

That influx of funds really got the ball rolling on the housing front in El Salvador, and then families began making the repayments that make the program sustainable. While the concept of paying mortgages is rather new for our homeowner partners, they quickly embrace it when they understand and feel the blessing of becoming givers themselves. Not only that, but their repayments often are less than what they were paying to rent shacks.

"Instead of living on dirt floors, these families get a whole new opportunity at life," Indiana State Sen. Jeff Raatz told us while gazing upon the 91 houses of Ahuachapán in 2022. "Not only that, it's theirs and they have to pay on a monthly basis, so they have some skin in the game. While that may seem harsh, the dignity connected with this really makes a difference in their lives. To bring these people up and out *and* make them part of the equation, to me, is incredible."

Acquiring land for these large communities and securing titles for families was not quite as simple as it is here in the United States. There were many hurdles. Fortunately, we made some powerful friends over the years who would go on to become even more powerful leaders and catalysts for change.

Michelle Sol was elected mayor of Nuevo Cuscatlán in 2015, and she embraced our work. She saw the impact that decent housing had for families who found themselves able to retain more of their income while having a base from which they could launch entrepreneurial endeavors, as well a place to raise their children where they could feel safe, be healthy, and excel in their studies. The mayor she succeeded was Nayib Bukele, another supporter of our work who would go on to be elected president in 2019. Michelle was re-elected mayor in 2018, but President Bukele wisely added her to his Cabinet in 2019 as his Minister of Housing. Their positive impact on the entire country cannot be overstated, and their support of our work has been tremendous. They have worked hard to remove obstacles and cut red tape. In fact, when I first met with Nayib before the election, I asked him how we could help him with his vision for El Salvador. He said he wanted us to do what we'd done for Nuevo Cuscatlán 262 more times— in every city across the country. After Michelle took office in the Cabinet, I asked her how we could help, and her reply was the same: *Do what you have done for Nuevo Cuscatlán 262 more times — in every city across El Salvador.* OK, maybe that's not quite so simple, but her point was clear. She wanted us to keep doing what we were doing, and she wanted our work to grow and spread. The administration has played a huge role in our rapid growth of homes and communities.

Photo by Todd Scoggins
David Snell and I listen as El Salvador's Minister of Housing, Michelle
Sol, tells 2022 Vision Trip participants about progress in the country
and future plans. Michelle has been a tremendous advocate for both The
People Helping People Network and The Fuller Center for Housing.

In fact, they even worked with our team in El Salvador — Gente Ayudando Gente — to accelerate construction of these large communities by allowing us to use prison labor. Many nonviolent offenders who are in the "trust" phases of their sentences have participated in the construction process — not only gaining skills that can help them reintegrate successfully into society when they leave prison but also getting a day reduced from their sentences for each day they work.

Redemption is one of the foundational principles of Christianity, and this is redemption in action. It also makes sense from a practical standpoint. It's a win-win-win-win situation — for the families in need of decent places to live, for us and our partner organizations as we seek to uplift and empower those families and communities, for the prisoners themselves, and for a government that is committed to reducing crime and recidivism rates. Like so much of what works with People Helping People, it's just good common sense.

PHP Network file photo
Homeowner families contribute "sweat equity" in the building of
their homes, helping them retain their dignity as they are not charity
cases but instead are full partners in the construction process.

"They help us move a lot faster in the construction process," said Marco Castro, Gente Ayudando Gente's Program Manager. "Of course, it's important for families to be part of the sweat equity. The first month when we start a new project, families have to put in hours on the project so that they can see the challenges that the rest of the construction people are going to face. We want them to understand the difficulty of building a home so that they can take care of it afterward."

And the families appreciate having their sweat equity complemented by the inmates.

"The families cook breakfast and lunch for the inmates," Castro added "Families are really conscious of the help they're getting, so they really invest in having good food for the inmates."

The end result of the donations, the sweat equity, the labor, the government cooperation, the volunteers and the repayment process is a simple, decent home. Fuller Center Vice President of International Programs Ryan Iafigliola calls it the "whole home" concept: At the very least, for a home to be considered "whole" it must be a permanent structure with cooking facilities, sanitation, water for cleaning and drinking, protection from weather and harmful pests, safe electricity and "love in the mortar joints."

The whole homes not only provide foundations for families to succeed, but they also serve as springboards for entrepreneurship. Each of these communities boasts businesses scattered throughout. Stores and pharmacies operate out of some of the homes. Mechanics welcome customers, and the air is filled with the tempting aromas of pupusas and tamales being cooked to be sold to fellow residents. The hum of sewing machines — most of which have been provided by The People Helping People Network— is a common sound.

Few things compare to the happiness I feel each time I walk down one of the streets in these communities. Older adults wave as you walk by. Children laugh and run to greet you. There is joy and peace and love. God's presence is palpable, and there is satisfaction in knowing that — as a People Helping People Network supporter, volunteer or leader — you had a little something to do with the success of this beautiful community. I am certainly not the only one who comes away emotionally overwhelmed.

"Walking through the community was like I'd gone back in time to 'Mister Rogers' Neighborhood,'" said Susie Blain, who visited Ahuachapan II in March of 2023 with four colleagues from Dr. John Orthodontics of Mount Pleasant, Michigan. "It was like it was 1965. I'm walking down this perfectly lovely street, and the people are loving. It was surreal."

My friend and long-time supporter Matt Gillette has made multiple trips to El Salvador and has seen many of these thriving communities emerge from what had once been an empty plot of land.

"Coming back over the years and seeing the progression of the community that's been formed there, it's really unbelievable to go from the blank slate to the community of the kids and the safety and everybody out playing," he said. "It just felt so cozy. You look at the kids and look at the families, they're happy. There's joy there."

The joy and sense of ownership enjoyed by each homeowner family is multiplied many times over as the entire community shares that unified feeling.

PHP Network file photo
Adults are not the only ones capable of contributing
"sweat equity" in the building of their homes.

"We don't build just houses — we build dignity," Dr. Elmore said. "That comes with the house. These people are very proud, and they feel very special that they're going to own a home when before all they could do was rent. Having a home was never in the equation. So now they're part of a community. They're part of something bigger than they are. They now have dignity."

There is one time of year when the community-wide joy is most striking— Christmastime. People Helping People Network supporter and visual guru Todd Scoggins has traveled the world documenting how people work to take care of God's people. He has captured thousands of amazing images of joy and pain, including hundreds in the People Helping People Network archives. If you have followed us on social media, received emails from us or visited our website, you've seen his amazing work — some of which also adorn the pages of this book. Even though he has witnessed so much through camera lenses, Todd seemed particularly moved while strolling the streets of Ahuachapán II in December of 2022. For a moment, he stepped out from behind the camera and let it rest by his side so that he could relish the moment.

"The porches were adorned with Christmas lights, and they were blinking and flashing — it was just a beautiful, peaceful night," Todd noted. "It was dusk, and I was just walking by myself down the streets. I kept thinking about how peaceful it is here. What a sense of community there is! There were kids running and playing and laughing. Moms were holding their babies on their front porches and saying 'hi' to one another and to us as we walked by.

"I thought to myself, 'I could live here, I could live in a community like this,' because there was such a sense of peace and community," he added. "And we hope for that. We pray for that. We pray that is the result for neighbors, especially with The Fuller Center for Housing with the neighborhoods The Fuller Center and People Helping People creates. We pray that not only is there safety and shelter — that basic need — but also the greater sense of community that develops from that. And then, from there, the Kingdom of God grows and thrives."

Photo by Chris Johnson
Homes in the Ahuachapán community are adorned
with Christmas lights in December of 2022.

Hunger Relief

Of all of the miracles Jesus performed in the Gospels, only one of them is told in each of the four Gospels of Matthew, Mark, Luke, and John. That is the Miracle of the Loaves and Fishes, where Jesus fed 5,000 people starting with just five loaves of bread and two small fish.

And there were leftovers!

Now, I have seen miracle after miracle through our work at The People Helping People Network but nothing like that — although I certainly have felt the love of God in our hands as we extended them to His people in need.

The fact that the Miracle of the Loaves and Fishes was notable to each of those New Testament Gospel writers tells me that the nourishment of our bodies is rather important to say the least. Those who are hungry can focus on little else and are more susceptible to illness — physical and mental.

Even those who enjoy the blessing of having a decent home cannot continue their journey of empowerment if they are hungry. Healthcare comes after hunger relief in our HOPE Equation, but we cannot accomplish our healthcare objectives if people are hungry because they understandably prioritize finding food for themselves and their families over getting proper health screenings, dental care and treatment for existing conditions. After healthcare in the HOPE Equation comes education. However, a child who is hungry cannot focus. Hunger relief is critical to everything else in the HOPE Equation.

It would be nice if we could go around multiplying bread and fish and vegetables and chickens with a wave of our hands. If God wanted us to have that power, He'd have blessed us with it. He does want our souls and bodies nourished, though. We seek to not only alleviate immediate hunger issues but also to foster programs and initiatives that address those needs going forward. We multiply our efforts not in a miraculous instant but in a practical process. And that process means partnering with those who are the best at delivering sustenance, such as our partners at World Food Program. President George W. Bush appointed my friend Jim Morris to lead the WFP, and they were a tremendous help in delivering food to the hungry in El Salvador and Guatemala during that time.

Photo by Chris Johnson
MaryAnn Kolb delivers some basic food items to a
resident of Juáyua in December 2022.

At The People Helping People Network, we aim to offer a hand-up instead of a handout and empower people to help themselves in the long run. But when hunger has taken hold and the danger is immediate, that is the time to hand out basic food items to get families through a crisis. It is a bridge to better days, not the permanent solution.

Our partners at Convoy of Hope are especially valuable in times of crisis. For instance, when Covid had El Salvador in its grasp in 2020, the country also faced a double-whammy from tropical storms Amanda and Cristobal. Food supplies went from short to almost completely depleted. In partnership with Convoy of Hope and the U.S. Department of Defense, The People Helping People Network delivered 64,000 pounds of food and hygiene kits in a C-17 cargo plane to the people of El Salvador, where it was received by then-U.S. Ambassador Ron Johnson, Convoy of Hope El

Salvador Director Winifred Patricia Mendez and our own Lisselot Troconis.

Our leaders on the ground in El Salvador at the Center for Hope do an incredible job of coordinating with organizations like Convoy of Hope and others to secure basic food items for families. By the year 2022, our team was distributing more than 2,100 pounds of black beans, 22,000 pounds of pork-n-beans, and 12,000 pounds of rice annually. Rice is not all that simple to put into perspective for those of us who are more likely to see rice as an occasional side dish, but 12,000 pounds of rice comes out to more than 86,000 servings.

Food distribution events are among the highlights of our People Helping People Network Vision Trips to El Salvador. Food is distributed throughout the year by our team on the ground, but during Vision Trips our participants help us deliver bags of basic foodstuffs like rice and cereal to families. This gives the people who support our work an opportunity to interact one-on-one with the people who benefit from their support. It is an opportunity for our supporters to let our food recipients know that they are loved, and it gives the families a chance to say, 'Gracias!"

I should note that during 2022, we also distributed 24,000 slices of pizza. Pizza is hardly a staple item, but it certainly delivers more smiles than any other food we deliver! In the spring of 2023, we visited Giusseppe Angelucci en Zaragoza Home for the Elderly for the first time. Run by a church, the home had very few resources. Their needs were numerous, but the residents longed for a treat from the outside — pizza. The joy on those faces when we came back with boxes of pizzas is something I'll never forget.

(A month later, by the way, PHP Network supporters helped us fund the delivery of many needed items to the home including a new refrigerator, freezer, microwave, clothes dryer, transfer benches for patients, crutches, canes, a walker, and gallons of soap, shampoo, body cream and more.)

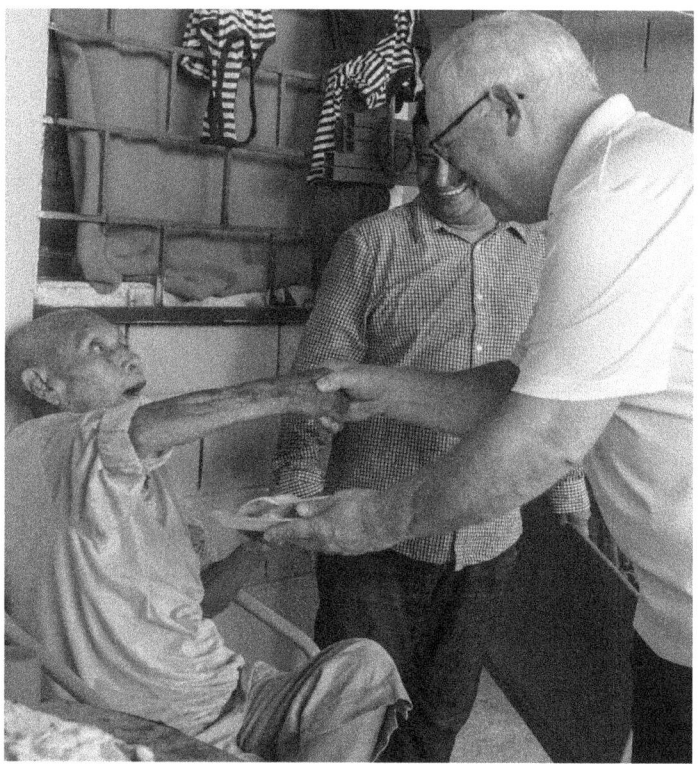

Photo by Todd Scoggins

What a joy it was to revisit the residents of Giusseppe Angelucci en Zaragoza Home for the Elderly and help distribute meals in June of 2023. This was a special side trip while attending the Congress of Honorary Consuls as the Honorary Consul of El Salvador in the United States, an honor given by the Bukele Administration in 2023.

Of course, giving away food is merely a stop-gap measure meant to get families over the hump or through a temporary situation. Ultimately, as with all of our programs, we want to give people the tools to help themselves. There are many ways to do this in the food arena, including by sharing farming tools, supplies, seeds, and expertise.

The donation of a hen may seem like a small thing, but it can be a big deal for a family when you consider that *one hen can lay more than 300 protein-rich eggs in a single year*. We can also multiply the gift of a hen through breeding, so that more egg-layers can benefit a whole village.

The gift of a decent stove can help a family produce more meals more safely and even provide a tool for entrepreneurship for those who seek to sell their dishes. These are just a few of the ways that hunger relief can be dealt with on a more long-term basis.

Then there's water. This doesn't fall neatly under the heading of hunger relief, but the situation is similar. Those who have no water need it now, just as those who have no food need it now. Many of our food deliveries and disaster responses involve the distribution of clean water, including in the United States after hurricanes and tornadoes. In El Salvador, the communities we build in conjunction with The Fuller Center for Housing prioritize providing a supply of clean, potable water. Clean water is sort of a thread that connects the second element of The HOPE Equation (hunger relief) and the third (healthcare).

During our 2017 Vision Trip to El Salvador, we visited the community of La Herradura, better known to our group as "Promise Land." The promise was new homes that would replace a collection of shacks in a community a few miles away.

"It was atrocious," recalled Mark Bowell, one of the trip participants. "They were in a wash area, and they had sewage and waste coming up in there."

A few families already had put up some rickety wooden houses in advance of the Fuller Center homes we would build in La Herradurra. They were desperate to escape the conditions at their previous area. Unfortunately, they had unleashed a new problem in trying to create a solution. They hand-dug water wells that were too shallow, and the water they retrieved from it was contaminated with pollutants from nearby sugar cane fields.

As we began walking in La Herradura where the new Fuller Center homes would soon rise, we met a family in a terrible state of despair, so different from the joyousness we were used to finding at every turn. They had just lost the patriarch of the family, whose internal organs had been damaged by the polluted water. Others in the community also were sick. The emotional scene really got to Mark, who had lost his oldest son to brain cancer just a few months earlier.

Photo by Todd Scoggins
Access to clean water inside the home is considered a luxury by most of our partner families, but we view it as necessary and fundamental for healthy families and communities.

"Obviously, the fragility of life was very impactful for me," Mark said. "These folks had just lost their husband, their father, and in many regards, they didn't know why."

After we met that family, The Fuller Center's David Snell said that what this community desperately needed was a properly dug well, which he noted would cost about $5,000. At that very moment back in the United States, the Bowen Family Foundation — started by Mark's in-laws — was having a meeting to determine upcoming charitable opportunities. Mark called his daughter at the meeting, and within minutes the well was funded.

"In 10 minutes we were able to go from David saying we needed a water well to having the money for the well," Mark remembered. "We were able to trigger the necessary funds at that very moment and deliver a miraculous blessing."

Mark and the foundation have since funded more wells for our communities, in addition to providing funding for our culinary school, air-conditioning for a cancer treatment facility and other initiatives. That all is in addition to their charitable outreach in the United States — much of which is focused on providing college scholarships for disadvantaged youth.

The homes we and our partners have been able to provide in places like La Herradura make an obvious difference that you can see. Having proper infrastructure such as proper sewers and safe, clean water is less visible but just as important in transforming these collections of houses into whole, thriving communities.

"They have water in their homes, and they have septic systems," Dr. Michael Elmore has noted. "I've always said that if you want to solve 90 percent of the health care problems in those places, give them bathroom facilities and give them clean water to drink. Our housing projects have done that. And People Helping People has a variety of medical services that continue to expand.

"We've always said that from an education standpoint that hungry kids living in a bad situation can't learn," he continued. "So now they're in their own safe home, and we've eliminated 90 percent of their health problems. Through the food program, we're making sure they're fed well, so now they can study and learn. When you look at the thousands of people who have moved into the homes, it completely transforms their lives. What has happened is sort of mind-blowing."

And that is merely the midway point of The HOPE Equation.

Healthcare

As Dr. Elmore has preached, when you provide safe housing, nutrition, clean water, and adequate sanitation, you already are well on your way to seeing healthier families and healthier communities. Those issues are crucial, but they may not help those facing other situations, such as cancer diagnoses or physical disabilities. Life is complicated enough for those in the developed world who are confronted with these situations, but it is far more difficult for people fighting these health battles in the third world.

Someone who is keenly aware of that truth is The People Helping People Network's very own Lisselot Troconis, who is without a doubt the single person who deserves the most credit for our success in El Salvador as she runs Gente Ayudando Gente with boundless energy, passion, enthusiasm, and the delicate mix of perseverance and patience it takes to navigate governmental bureaucracies and get things accomplished in a third-world environment.

Lisselot knew that among the most pressing needs on the healthcare front were screening and prevention tools, especially for the rampant cases of breast cancer in the country, where far too many cancers were being detected far too late. The People Helping People Network delivered its first ultrasonography machine to the Center for Hope in November of 2010.

However, there was an unexpected issue: Women were unfamiliar with screenings and sonograms. The machine was intimidating. Lisselot and a few friends decided that the best way to alleviate fears was to get sonograms themselves. Lisselot was the last to get one, agreeing only after her friends ratted her out to the doctor as "the only one who hasn't done it." She reluctantly obliged so that she could get it out of the way and move on with her business. Instead, the ultrasound discovered a concerning spot. A biopsy determined it to be non-cancerous, but the doctor wanted to revisit the area with an ultrasound within three months … just to be safe.

Two months later, Lisselot went in for what she thought would be a routine screening to confirm that, indeed, all was well. It was not. That spot they thought was innocuous had grown 50 percent into a scary tumor. A second biopsy confirmed that it was cancerous. It was definitely not the news she hoped to hear, but she thought it might be divine intervention.

"I said, 'God, if you're giving me this so I will know how these ladies feel when they come in here, then I'll take this,'" Lisselot remembered. Although, she gave God a little advice: "But don't overdo it with me because I'm not that strong.

Photo by Todd Scoggins
Lisselot Troconis enjoys a dance with husband Oscar at a 2022 Gente Ayudando Gente/People Helping People gala in San Salvador.

"Thank God it was very, very early," she added. "I had a good treatment with no side effects from the chemo except that I lost my hair. But I had wigs."

(Note: Hundreds of people have donated their hair in recent years to be used in making wigs for the cancer patients we assist.)

Because Lisselot is a survivor, she has become a walking testament to the importance of early detection. Over the next decade-plus, more than 10,000 women would be screened. Hundreds of those who were found to have cancers would go on to receive ImmunoHistoChemistry kits provided by The People Helping People Network. IHCs are used to determine the exact type of cancer so that doctors can select the proper course of treatment and medicines.

"The ladies used to just start with a basic drug, do six months of chemotherapy, and then what happened?" Lisselot said. "It came back. They need to know what kind of cancer it is so they know what kind of chemo they need. Otherwise, they just know it's breast cancer."

Fortunately, the government has taken notice of the successful treatments made possible by the IHC kits.

"After we began providing kits, the government started getting their own," Lisselot said. "So we were able to make a start. Now the ladies have the ImmunoHistoChemistry kits, and they're able to know what kind of medicine they need and are not going back so often."

Another woman who benefited from early detection was Lizzy, who discovered she had cancer on the very same day she also learned that she was preg-

PHP Network file photo
At age 32, Lizzy found out she was pregnant and that she had breast cancer. She was urged to abort her baby, then turned to us. We helped her get safe treatment while pregnant. Today, Lizzy is a survivor and her daughter is happy and healthy.

nant. Some doctors suggested that she would need mega-aggressive treatments — and that she would need to abort the baby so that she could get started immediately. Lizzy was devastated. She refused to give up her baby. She came to us in a desperate state, and we were able to help her plot an effective course of treatment that was safer for her and her baby. Today, Lizzy is a survivor, and that baby she refused to give up is a happy, healthy girl with a beautiful smile.

Lizzy was 32 when that cancer was detected. That age is notable because our screenings have uncovered a disturbing trend in El Salvador: Half of those cancers have been found in Salvadoran women aged 32 and younger.

"That includes teenagers," Lisselot noted. "The younger the girl, the more difficult it is because it's very aggressive and often comes back."

Without early detection programs, Salvadorans might not have been aware of that disturbing trend. While no one has yet been able to explain why this is, the first step toward solving a problem is to identify it. As the years go on, early detection grows in its importance.

PHP Network file photo

Preparing support boxes at the Center for Hope
for distribution to cancer patients.

After detection, their treatment is in the hands of doctors, whom we have helped better understand the situation through our proactive initiatives. But we do not simply "hand off" the women who have been screened. Thousands of women have had counseling sessions at the Center for Hope to help them through the process, and young women and girls in the community have eagerly supported them by donating their hair to make wigs. We did have a dormitory for women to rest after treatements, but hospitals have since taken notice and are now addressing the vital need for rest themselves, allowing us to use the former dormitory space for the expansion of other programs. As each year passes and more People Helping People Network supporters meet these women and see the facilities, more services are able to be provided.

Of course, our healthcare initiatives reach far beyond cancer screenings and support. Another important early intervention issue is dental care, also all too rare in the Salvadoran communities we serve — until now.

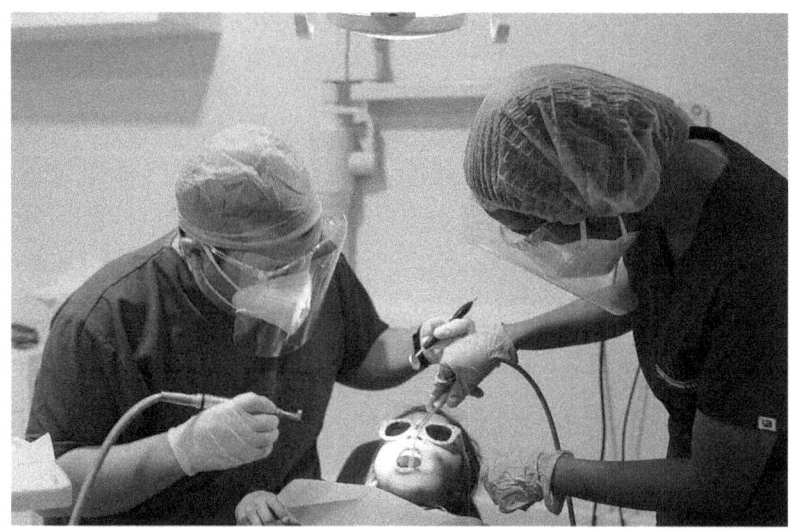

PHP Network file photo
Dr. Jose Mixco and Sarah Linares treat a young patient
at the Center for Hope's dental clinic.

The Center for Hope has a state-of-the-art dental clinic. It is small, but it always is fun to me to watch supporters as they see it for the first time because it looks as high-tech and well-equipped as any office you might find in the United States. It is obvious by the stunned looks on their faces that they expected something completely different.

At the helm of this clinic is Dr. Jose Mixco, Lisselot's son.

"I've worked in rural areas, so I know that people here do need a lot of dental work," said Jose, who started the clinic in 2021. "I even did a study with kids ages 6-9 and saw that at least 70 percent have a cavity in their first permanent molars — a cavity that might lead to an extraction or at least a root canal."

Today, the clinic sees about 1,000 patients a year. The team also hits the road as it goes into communities with a mobile clinic where they provide basic exams and treatments, as well as distributing dental care supplies from The People Helping People Network.

In March of 2023, Dr. John Yurkovich of Dr. John Orthodontics of Mount Pleasant, Michigan, along with three members of his team, joined us on a trip to El Salvador so that they could further enhance the smiles of children with braces. Lisselot's orthodontist daughter Lisse Mixco de Brito and her company, The Smile Factory of El Salvador, provided follow-up care.

That our clinic has gone from treating basic dental issues to building beautiful smiles is a testament to the expertise on the ground there and the support from here in the U.S., especially from those in the field like Dr. John.

"They were so helpful, and we kind of just came together as a team," Dr. John said of our team at the Center for Hope. "Usually it takes about an hour and a half or two hours to do it, but with all of the teamwork, we were able to put braces on in an hour. We were able to do 22 people. It was a pretty incredible experience."

The families they assisted thought it was pretty incredible, too.

"They were unbelievably grateful," Dr. John said. "They were so excited to pick out the colors of their braces. Some people got teary after they saw them. Some of the parents couldn't say thank you enough.

"It definitely gave me a sense of perspective of just how different life is here," he added. "It gave me a sense of gratitude and a sense of excitement — excitement to go back and excitement to see how the treatments are progressing. Overall, it's just gratefulness."

There are many other areas of healthcare in which The People Helping People Network is involved (including providing supplies to health clinics, mental hospitals, elderly care homes and an orphanage). In 2005, we teamed up with Dr. Rajiv Sood and began raising funds to build the first and only pediatric burn center in El Salvador. Opened in 2010, it is the only such burn center in Central America.

But there is one area that generates more smiles, hugs, and tears of joy than any other — wheelchair distribution.

Nearly everyone who goes on a Vision Trip will tell you that one of the most memorable things about it — usually the most memorable — is our wheelchair giveaways. These events begin with our participants assembling wheelchairs we obtain from our partners at Free Wheelchair Mission at a much lower cost than the used wheelchairs we would buy in the early days of the program. The chairs are then lined up and numbered for each recipient who will soon arrive. The room goes silent for a moment when people of various conditions and disabilities are helped into the room.

PHP Network file photo

Todd Scoggins steps out from behind the camera
to meet a grateful wheelchair recipient.

Some of the chairs barely roll. Most are ill-fitting or far too small. Others are held together with twine and plastic. Occasionally, a person has to be carried in someone's arms. I've witnessed these arrivals dozens of times, and it is always heartbreaking for me to see what they have had to endure, especially the older folks. I know that those who witness it for the first time are almost immediately brought to tears of excruciating empathy.

One by one, we help these long-suffering people move to their new wheelchairs — sturdy, attractive and dependable. You can see the relief in their eyes. Our Vision Trip participants' tears of empathy transform into tears of joy. Quite frankly, when these events come early in a Vision Trip, some of the participants wonder if they will be able to handle the emotional roller-coaster of a few days in El Salvador.

"In America, wheelchairs are accessible," PHP supporter Matt Gillette said. "They're everywhere. You don't think twice about it. Here, getting a wheelchair is almost like hitting the lottery for someone who's in need.

Some of these people have never had a wheelchair in their entire life. Others had wheelchairs held together with rope and twine.

"Having the families come and being able to bless and pray over them for this change in their lifestyle — not just their lifestyle but their family's lifestyle — that's a really, really big deal," he added. "Being a small part of that, gosh, it's pretty impactful."

That is what Matt told us in December of 2022 as we began our first full day of that Vision Trip with a morning wheelchair give-away. He had been on multiple Vision Trips. However, his friend MaryAnn Kolb was with us for the very first time. The entire trip was deeply emotional for her, but the wheelchair distribution was especially moving.

"My father was in a wheelchair, and I know what it was like to give him mobility and a sense of independence," MaryAnn told us. "The fact that we were able to bring that to the elders and young children was beyond anything I've ever experienced before. For those people who've never had a wheelchair, it transforms their life, and I'm grateful to have been a part of that transformation process."

When I think about how the simple but important gift of a wheelchair changes lives, two women — Eeileen Romero and Wendy Caishpal.

I received one of the greatest honors in my life in 2019 when El Salvador's Congress bestowed upon me the title "Noble Friend of El Salvador," the highest honor the body gives to people from outside the country. I had the opportunity to address the Congress and advocate for The People Helping People Network's uplifting and empowering nonprofit work. Afterward, many of the representatives came up to meet me, shake my hand, thank me, and pose for photos. In other words, it was a special day but fairly standard procedure for such an occasion.

Photo by Todd Scoggins

When I received the El Salvadoran Congress' highest honor for a non-citizen — Noble Friend of El Salvador — in 2019, Rep. Eeileen Romero came to the floor to thank me for a wheelchair we had sent years ago: "This wheelchair changed my entire life. Prior to this, I was homebound." She would go on to get her law degree and was elected to Congress in 2018. She died in 2021.

Then Eeileen came up to speak with me. Well, actually, she rolled up to meet me. Eeileen was born in 1974 with brittle bone disease, evidenced by seven fractures suffered during her birth. She lost her father to El Salvador's Civil War when she was just 8 years old, and she did not get the chance to attend school until she was 13. She made the most of her late schooling opportunities and went on to further her education in college, ultimately achieving a law degree. The Supreme Court of Justice appointed her Lawyer of the Republic of El Salvador in 2008. In 2018, she was elected to Congress and served until April 30 of 2021.

"Hey, do you recognize this?" Eeileen asked me. "This is one of the wheelchairs that you'd shipped down earlier. I'd never had a wheelchair, ever, in my life. I just wanted to say thank you to you and your team for providing wheelchairs. This wheelchair changed my entire life. Prior to this, I was homebound."

I teared up. I didn't think anything could top being named Noble Friend of El Salvador. However, few things can compare to seeing someone's life transformed as significantly as Eeileen's was. She became a representative of the people, and she spent her remaining days on this earth advocating for rights and opportunities for the disabled. She died of cardiac arrest on October 25, 2021.

Wendy Caishpal, meanwhile, is the founder of Ahuchapán Sin Baarreras or Ahuachapán Without Barriers, which promotes and protects the rights of all people, especially the disabled. They also are a key partner in our wheelchair initiatives. Wendy was there with Matt and MaryAnn and others on our December 2022 vision trip, as usual, to organize the wheelchair distribution — and to inspire the entire room as she does it all from her own wheelchair.

When Wendy was 14, she lost her mobility when gunmen attacked the car in which she was riding with a cousin who was delivering bread. Her cousin was shot in the head and killed, while she was hit five times, leaving her in a coma for two weeks. After a long rehabilitation, she furthered her education and got her law degree. Though she could no longer walk, she had an adequate wheelchair for which she was thankful. However, she knew many others in El Salvador could not say the same.

Today, she says she is grateful for the tragedy that befell her as a teenager because it has spawned a cause that has helped hundreds enjoy mobility and independence. Can you imagine the determination and perspective it requires to be *thankful* for having been shot and confined to a wheelchair for the rest of your life?!

What Wendy started in Ahuachapán is now helping people in at least 24 communities across El Salvador. They help People Helping People distribute about 200 wheelchairs per year and would love to do more.

"It's a great alliance between the organizations," Wendy said of Ahuachapán Without Barriers, Free Wheelchair Mission and The People Helping People Network. "And this is a day to feel useful. It's an opportunity to change the lives of these people. It provides the opportunity for mobility and independence because in this seat they can actually move around."

Photo by Todd Scoggins
Wendy Caishpal poses with Kathy Carrier, one of the 2022 Vision Trip participants who helped us assemble wheelchairs that were distributed to those in need later that morning.

During that December 2022 visit, everyone had the opportunity to meet Wendy. And Lizzy. And Lisse. And Jose. And Lisselot. And every single wheelchair recipient. These experiences with people who have been changed through our healthcare initiatives and those who are carrying out the changes are emotionally intense. They are as draining as they are uplifting.

And they are unforgettable.

Education

When most people think about the word education, they think about pencils, paper, books, and other such basic school supplies. We indeed deliver many such items throughout El Salvador and in some U.S. communities. Those are most definitely important. But we look at education as any tool or training that provides the kind of learning or knowledge a person requires in order to obtain higher educational outcomes or better career prospects.

Perhaps no element of The HOPE Equation more illustrates hope than the education factor. Housing, hunger relief and healthcare are crucial parts of the equation, but those needs are more immediate. The education component is about the future, not the *now*. When people believe they have a future, they have hope. And hope is the one thing none of us can live without. We can *talk* about hope. We can *preach* about hope. But when we provide educational opportunities, we see hope in the eyes of those who eagerly seize the opportunity to better their current situation. You can see that hope not just in the eyes of students in schools and children in orphanages but also in the eyes of adults training for careers so that they can better support their families and those in prison who are determined to not only avoid going back to jail but who also want to thrive and be productive members of society.

San Vicente de Paul Orphanage is a frequent stop on our Vision Trips to El Salvador, especially in December when we deliver Christmas gifts. But supporting the hard-working sisters and teachers of the orphanage *yearround* with basic supplies and donations is what helps make their educational efforts successful over the long haul. When many of our first-time Vision Trip participants approach the doors of the orphanage, I can feel their trepidation. It's as if they

are bracing themselves for a wave of sadness, despair and hopelessness. No one wants to see a child sad or without hope.

What they find, however, is the exact opposite. Children are
not just learning — they are doing so *joyfully*. There are smiles and
laughter at every turn. They *love* learning. They love each other like
one big family. And they are quick to share their abundant love with
the visitors who come bearing gifts and supplies.

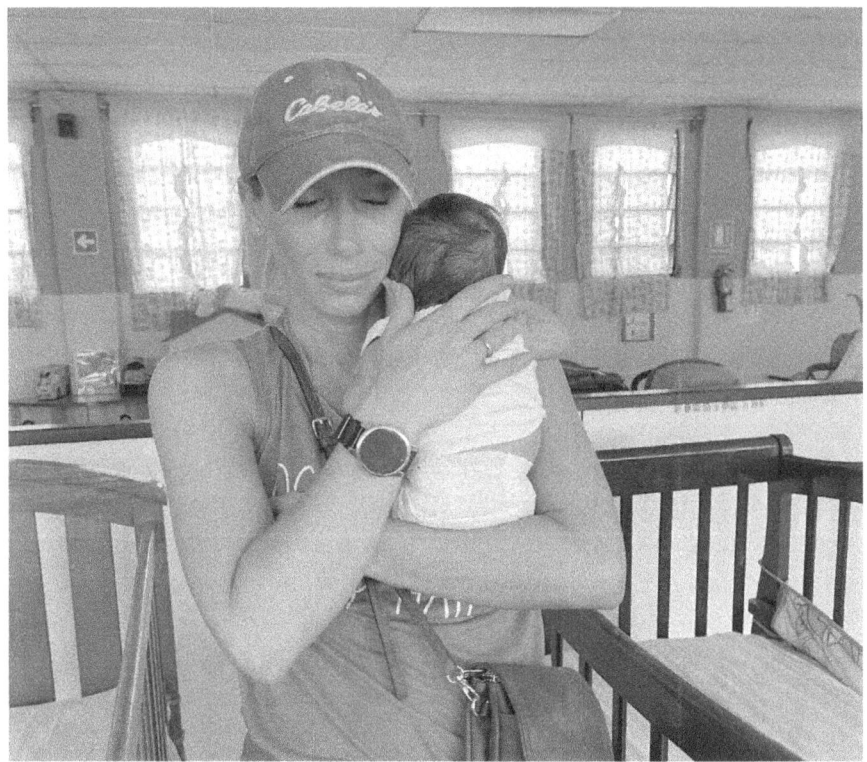

PHP Network file photo
Susie Blain holds a baby at San Vicente de Paul Orphanage in March 2023.

"It all comes from love," Beatrice, secretary to the orphanage's
director, told us. "You can work here for one of two reasons — money
or love. But I can tell you that all of the people here who work with
the kids are here for love. That love is shown day in and day out, and
that makes a huge difference. And we are so grateful for the blessings

of the visitors and the donations. It means a lot to the kids and to the people who work here."

"It is always most memorable going to the orphanage," Rich Van Paris said in December 2022 after visiting as a board member on the Vision Trip. "You look in these little children's eyes anywhere from newborns to 17 or 18 years old, and you wonder why they've been orphaned, and that's the sad part.

"But the joyous part is that they are in an extremely healthy and safe environment, they're going to have basic skills when they move up to the 18-year-old level and graduate and be gainfully employed," he added. "You see no sadness with any of these children. They don't know what they don't have. They appreciate everything they've got. The sisters of San Vicente de Paul have a wonderful foundation to build upon for 18 years.

They do a great job."

Among the many other places where we help facilitate educational opportunities and vocational training is in El Salvador's prison system. There are some facilities filled with dangerous gang members and violent criminals. However, there are others where prisoners have committed nonviolent offenses, often the result of bad decision-making stemming from the desperation to support their families. That does not justify criminal behavior, but these are people who will be returned to the community. When they are released, they are likely to fall back into the same desperate cycle unless they have opportunities to legitimately support their families. Prisoners nearing the completion of their sentences are tremendously grateful for the hope that training and educational opportunities provide.

Not only do they benefit as individuals, but so do their families and the communities in which they live. By reducing recidivism in this way, we also help the government focus energies on eradicating major criminal activities. I feel far safer these days walking the streets of El Salvador than I do in many American cities.

One of those prison training programs is the one I mentioned in the housing section of The HOPE Equation — using inmate labor to help build homes. These inmates in the "trust" phase toward the end of their sentences not only get one day trimmed from their sentences for each day that they work, but they receive valuable construction training as they work on multiple phases of house building. This greatly increases their chances of finding gainful employment when they are released. In fact, some of them have even been hired as laborers by our own Gente Ayudando Gente team in the country. They have become trusted workers who not only can support their families but also play a role in improving their community..

Our culinary school at the Center for Hope has become more
successful than we could have ever hoped for, and graduates
of the program have a 95 percent job placement rate.

No training program, though, has taken off quite like our culinary school, which is housed at the Center for Hope in San Salvador. We thought it was a fun idea to offer training in the culinary arts so that a few students could pursue careers as chefs, bakers, baristas, and such. No one could have predicted how many people would jump at the opportunity to learn culinary skills, nor how many supporters the program would have from both the United States and within El Salvador. Americans have stepped up to provide scholarships for students to complete certificate courses, while the hospitality industry in El Salvador has stepped up to the plate, pun intended, as well. Restaurants and hotels are now jumping at the opportunity to work with the culinary school's students through a new program that adds a fourth month to the formerly three-month course in which students get hands-on practice in a commercial environment.

"In the culinary school right now, we're talking to the biggest restaurants in El Salvador," Gente Ayudando Gente Program Director Marco Castro said. "They're really interested in getting scholarships for our students for a fourth month, giving them an opportunity in their kitchens so that they can practice with their staff — and after that often being hired full-time. We're talking to hotels, restaurants and chain restaurants."

The program is hardly just a way for people to brush up on cooking skills. It trains people for careers in the culinary industry. And it must train them quite well because it has a 95 percent job placement rate for its graduates.

The People Helping People Network also has incorporated psychological support and counseling for students, many of whom have never had the opportunity to hold down a formal job.

Of course, you can't have great students without a great teacher, and that is one of the blessings that helped catapult the school from a cool idea to a thriving vocational training program. José Rodriguez is the

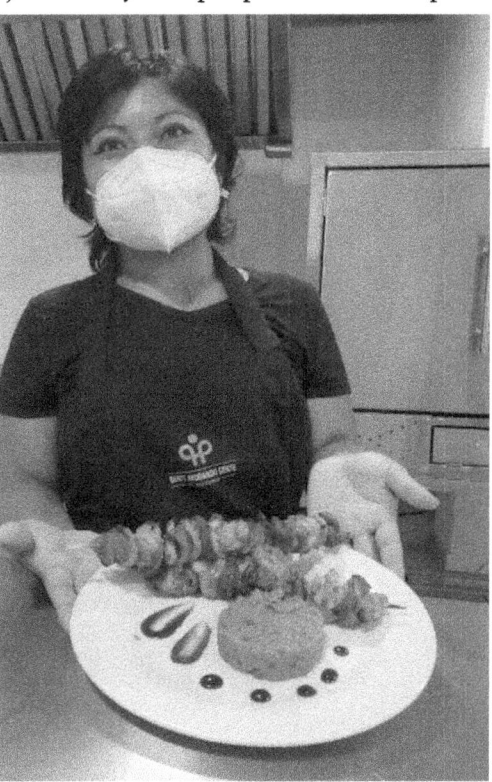

PHP Network file photo
Carla has benefited from the breast cancer support services and the culinary school at the Center for Hope..

master chef who commands attention with a reserved but demanding demeanor in the class kitchen at People Helping People's headquarters in San Salvador. We originally started out working with him hoping he would simply help us build a curriculum and help us get things up and started and maybe train a team to get going. But he has enjoyed it so much that he continues to lead the program, and he loves teaching these students. He has a passion for teaching people to be chefs and helping people to get employment.

Many of our culinary students are connected to other elements of The HOPE Equation. For instance, Carla was 26 years old when she found herself battling breast cancer a second time despite having had a double-mastectomy during her first battle. We provided her monthly cancer medication free of charge and helped her get back on her feet with a scholarship for the culinary program. She now supports herself and daughter by cooking and selling food from her home.

(As of 2023, you could sponsor a four-month scholarship at the culinary school for just $300.)

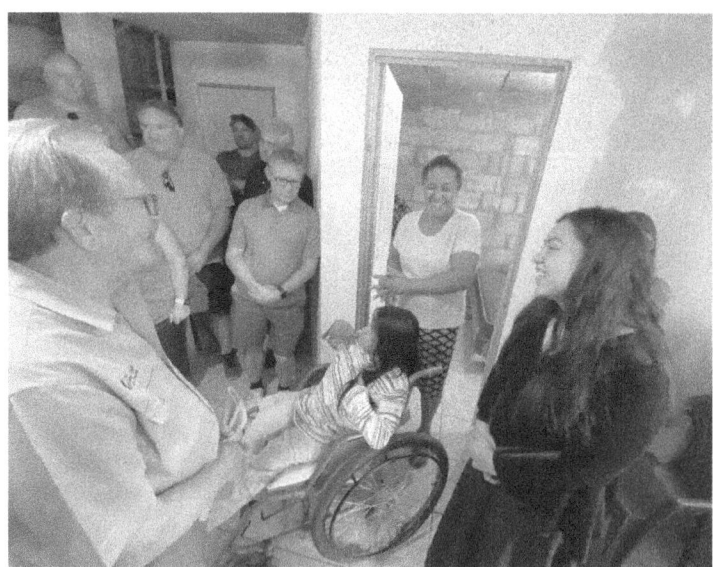

Photo by Chris Johnson

The de Grandes family has benefited from all four components of The HOPE Equation — housing, hunger relief, healthcare, and education. They eagerly welcomed Vision Trip participants into their new home in December 2022, and we had an impromptu second house blessing for the family.

Not far from the school in the 131-home community of Nuevo Cuscatlán II, one of the first homeowner partners was Gabriela. Before she got the keys to her new Fuller Center home, we met her in her old house on a hill. Her youngest daughter Andrea is confined to a wheelchair and unable to speak. She rarely left the house, and if she did, Gabriela had to carry Andrea's rickety wheelchair up 90 treacherous steps to the house. She would do this alone most of the time because her husband is a hard-working farmer who is rarely home during daylight hours.

We helped Andrea get a new wheelchair, and Gabriela became a student in the first-ever class at our culinary school, and she has since become an expert tamale-maker. They now have a new Fuller Center home, and Gabriela is able to prepare tamales from the home's kitchen. Older daughter Stephanie sells in the community when she is not studying Business Administration at college on a scholarship sponsored by a Fuller Center Global Builders volunteer from Ireland who met the family while working alongside them to build their new home. The de Grande family was so excited about the new house that they did not wait for the final touches to be made before moving in. Neighbors had to rush to do a home blessing for the de Grandes, whom they all love and knew how important it was for them to have a simple, decent place to live and care for their family, especially Andrea.

When we visited the family in their new home in December 2022, our Vision Trip participants were packed shoulder-to-shoulder as Gabriela told her story with the most grateful smile. Stephanie entered in the middle of the chaos with a beautiful smile of her own. Andrea sat in her wheelchair and made almost no sound until we prayed over the home with the family, an impromptu second home blessing. When we finished praying and everyone said, "Amen!" Andrea squealed with delight. I have rarely seen so much of our equation so joyously represented in a single moment like this one.

This home, this family epitomizes what we're all about — extending a hand-up to wonderful families and empowering them to build better lives for themselves and future generations. The de Grande family is so grateful for their many blessings, but People Helping People Network supporters are the ones who have received the Greater Blessing by making it all possible.

Multiplied by faith!

While housing, hunger relief, healthcare and education are the practical pillars upon which The HOPE Equation is built, it is that final part of the equation — "multiplied by faith" — that King's Castle Ministries' Don Triplett says is the key component.

"I love People Helping People because there's a place for people who have resources to be able to help people, but at the same time there's a place for God to touch people as they're helping people," he said. "It makes all the difference."

Faith is not just an accelerant that ignites the success of The HOPE Equation, but it also is a bonding element that brings people together. It brings people of all walks of life and philosophies together to share God's love, something they can all agree upon just as they all agree on helping people to help themselves. As Millard Fuller notably paraphrased James 2:26 from the Bible with his trademark Southern drawl: "Faith without works is as dead as a doornail!" He called it "The Theology of the Hammer," and we follow it today — with hammers, wheelchairs, rice, training courses, school supplies, and so much more. The root of our philosophy is the same as Millard's — we just require a bigger toolbox!

"The Theology of the Hammer simply means that as Christians we will agree on the use of the hammer as an instrument to manifest God's love," The Fuller Center's David Snell explains. "We may disagree on all sorts of other things — baptism, communion, what night to have prayer meetings, and how the preacher should dress — but we can agree on the imperative of the Gospel to serve others in the name of the Lord."

Fuller family photo

Millard Fuller preached the Theology of the Hammer, putting faith into action.

PHP Network file photo

From left: My son Jeffery, myself, and Fuller Center President
David Snell delivering Spanish-language Bibles in 2022.
We also present Bibles at each house blessing.

Expressing that faith through action produces tangible results that you can see — safe homes instead of shacks, healthier people, joyous smiles, thriving entrepreneurship, and such. But sharing God's love impacts people in many ways that are less visible — including, and maybe even especially, for those who are doing the sharing.

During our March 2023 visit to the orphanage at San Vicente de Paul, we were joined by a contingent of eight students and three teachers from the Crossing School of Business and Entrepreneurship of Frankfort, Indiana. It was the first time most had been to any place even resembling a third-world country, and there were many moving moments that stuck with the teenagers on the trip. Then-senior Kylie Field remembers a special encounter that her teacher and trip leader Zach Golden had with an 11-yearold boy at the school. Zach used an English-to-Spanish translation app on his phone to chat with the young man and asked him what he would want if he could have anything in the world. The boy replied that he would ask God to remove the evil in the world.

"When I was an 11-year-old girl, I never would have said that," said Field, who added that she is now more determined than ever to share her faith. "When I first got back from the trip, it was real hard on me because a lot of the people around here in Indiana, they didn't understand what I saw, and trying to communicate it to people was really hard. I just wanted to spread the word about God so much. It was hard because a lot of my family isn't like me, and some of my friends don't know who God is. So, any chance I get I'm talking about God, and the old me didn't used to do that."

Also on that trip were Dr. John Yurkovich and three staff members from Dr. John Orthodontics of Mount Pleasant, Mich. While three of them spent most of their time at the Center for Hope helping children get braces, patient coordinator Susie Blain saw all aspects of The HOPE Equation in action, along with those students and the handful of other adults, including myself, who were leading them. As with most people who witness so much in such a short period of time, she was deeply touched and moved spiritually.

"It was breathtaking and awe-inspiring," Blain said. "It was all I could do to take it all in through the whole experience. It was just unlike anything that I've ever seen before. It was emotional and sometimes emotionally exhausting but in a good way because I could see something that I'd never seen or experienced before."

She was with the group as they distributed wheelchairs at a mental hospital and a home for the elderly — two places that PHP had never visited before this trip. It felt very different to her than being in similar American facilities.

"Because of HIPPA and what-not and different belief systems, here we're not able to go into a hospital and pray over people and be welcomed," Blain said. "People are skeptical, and there they were so grateful and just welcomed us. There were tears and people singing and grateful prayer. It was just something like I've never seen before.

PHP Network file photo
People Helping People Network supporters pray over
wheelchair recipients in March 2023..

"It was really incredible and life-changing for sure," she continued. "It's something that I couldn't have imagined. I came away with a renewed sense of faith and renewed sense of hope in humanity that has been kind of lost here in the States over the last few years because of all the things that our country has been going through."

The Crossing School's campus administrator, Marissa Mills, expressed similar feelings.

"Everything we did was about people," she said. "We went from one location to the next where we could just hug people, talk to people and encourage people. For me, that was very impactful. Love is a language, and we were able to connect in that way. I really enjoyed being able to pray in different spots. I don't feel like we do that in the United States very well."

Faith runs deep in El Salvador. The term "El Salvador" translates to "The Savior," so I guess a strong sense of faith throughout the country is to be expected. And where there is faith, there is joy. Those who visit El

Photo by Chris Johnson
Joyous children of the Juáyua community race while People Helping People Network supporters look on in December 2022.

Salvador with us marvel at the abundant joy Salvadorans show, whether they live in a sparkling new home or are still in a shack waiting for their moment to seize a hand-up to a brighter future.

"They're happy to see us, and they have joy even though they know their living conditions are not good," PHP Network supporter Kathy Carrier said. "It tells me that it's not things that give us joy — it's peace and family and God."

"I can't believe how friendly and nice everyone is," supporter Jodi Lewis added. "They've been unbelievable. There's joy and happiness here that we don't have in the United States. They're very appreciative, and I love them."

"People can still have joy whether they have a lot or a little," noted Pastor David Hull. "They're very appreciative of every little thing we do for them. Then we come to America and sometimes we're not as appreciative of what God's blessed us with. It's a joy to bless them because they appreciate everything. They have a very joyful spirit."

At The People Helping People Network, our faith is enhanced through our efforts, and so is *our* joy. For everything that we give, we get so much more in return. I guess it is just further verification of one of the best known verses in the entire Bible, from the book of Acts: *Hay más dicha en dar que en recibir.*

At least, that is the way it reads in the Spanish-language Bibles provided by our partners at Mission Cry that we distribute throughout El Salvador and give to families at each home blessing. Perhaps you know it better in English, "It is more blessed to give than to receive."

This little boy was so grateful for the Bible that he
received during an August 2022 visit.

Join us!

The country of El Salvador has been the proving ground for The People Helping People Network's HOPE Equation. It could have been another country facing a multitude of needs and problems. Each time I return to that prayer tower at King's Castle Ministries, though, I know more and more that the idea of my working in El Salvador was someone else's plan. I believe it was set in motion long before my daughter Sara dragged me on that mission trip with my wife practically shoving me out the door. God bless them both for their efforts. And I thank God that He used them — and countless others — to put me in the right place at the right time.

More than two decades later, however, we have honed The HOPE Equation. A few ideas did not take off, but the vast majority did — usually beyond our wildest dreams. Again, that's what happens when you multiply our practical formula by faith. With God, all things are possible.

The HOPE Equation can work in more places, and our efforts to spread God's love are hardly confined to El Salvador. We are based in Indianapolis, Indiana — my home. We continue to step forward after natural disasters here in the United States, often sending truckloads of supplies donated by local residents, businesses, and churches to places like Southwest Florida after Hurricane Ian and to Kentucky after the December 2021 tornadoes. We support Phalen Leadership Academies' Music for Success program by purchasing violins, violas, cellos, and double basses as they promote learning through music. We have annual toy drives to bring a little Christmas joy to children in need. We have supported difficult-but-important missions led by retired Army Maj. Gen. David L. Grange to evacuate Americans from Afghanistan (after the U.S. withdrawal) and help orphans in Ukraine.

The more support we have from people like you — through your generous gifts, your prayers, and your most precious gift of time spent with us — the more we can do, not just in El Salvador but in other lands where God's people desperately need hope.

If you would like to help us deliver that hope — to El Salvador, to American communities, and to more of God's people in need — please visit our website at **phpnetwork.org**.

Scrapbook

There are literally thousands of photographs related to our nonprofit work in El Salvador and the United States within The People Helping People Network's archives. Our partners, volunteers, supporters and friends have thousands more images that help tell our success stories. Over the next 10 pages, you will find a tiny fraction of some of those images that help us tell the story of The People Helping People Network and The HOPE Equation.

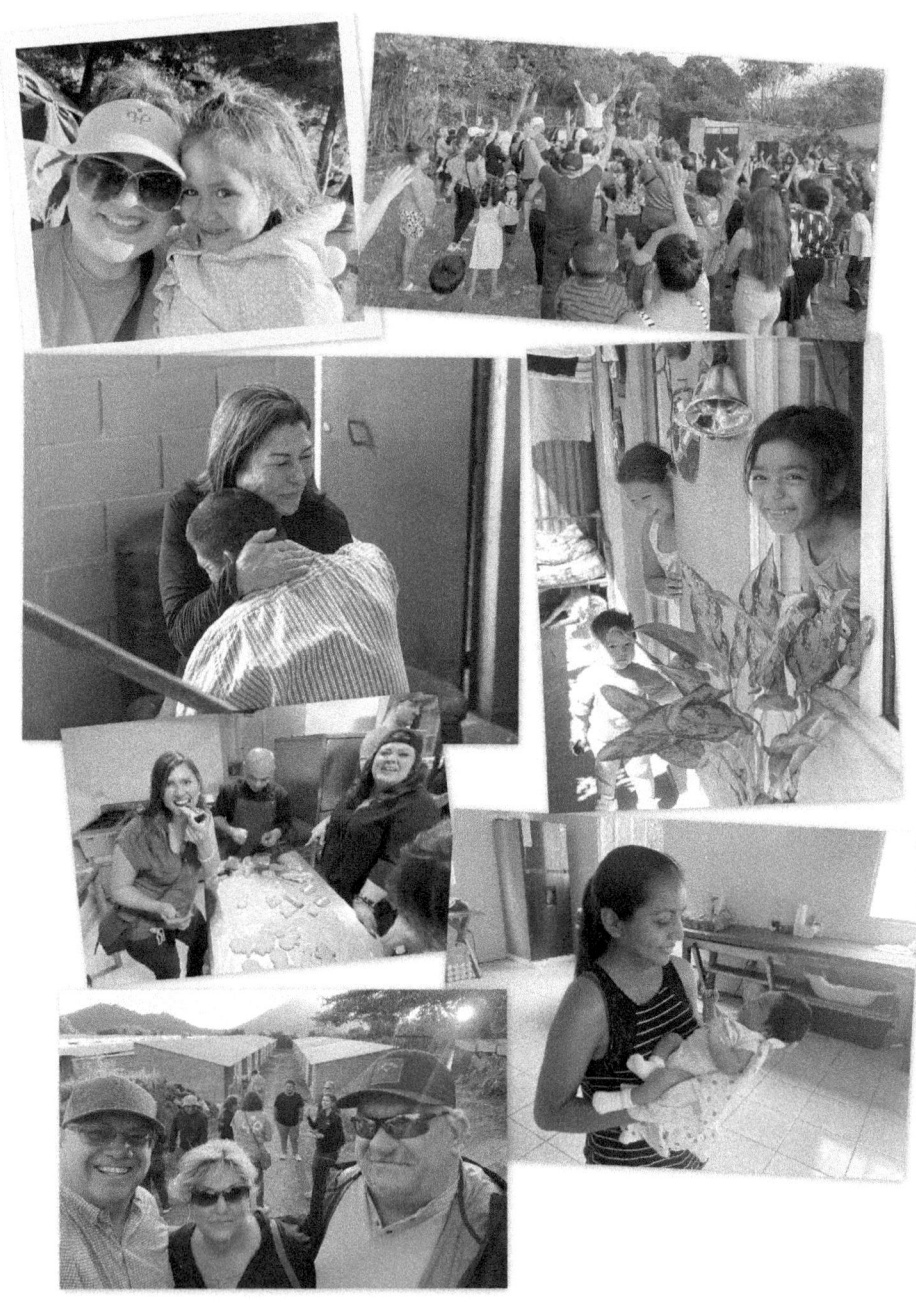

(Left to Right) Jeff Cardwell, Honorary Consul of El Salvador
and Nayib Bukele, President of El Salvador.

"Let God change you,
and you can change the world."
Cheryl Cardwell

www.ingramcontent.com/pod-product-compliance
Lightning Source LLC
Chambersburg PA
CBHW051229120626
46547CB00013B/1574

www.ingramcontent.com/pod-product-compliance
Lightning Source LLC
Chambersburg PA
CBHW051220120626
46547CB00013B/1434